Fisher-Price ®

PRESCHOOL WORKBOOK

WATCH ME LEARN

MODERN PUBLISHING
A Division of Unisystems, Inc.
New York, New York 10022

NOTE TO PARENTS

Dear Parents:

Helping your children master their world through early learning is as easy as the Fisher-Price® Workbooks!

As your child's first and most important teacher, you can encourage your child's love of learning by participating in learning activities at home. Working together on the activities in each of the Fisher-Price® Preschool Workbooks will help your child build confidence, learn to reason, and develop reading, writing, math and language skills.

Help make your time together enjoyable and rewarding by following these suggestions:

- Choose a quiet time when you and your child are relaxed.
- Provide a selection of writing materials (pens, pencils, or crayons).
- Discuss each page. Help your child relate the concepts in the books to everyday experiences.
- Only work on a few pages at a time. Don't attempt to complete every page if your child becomes tired or loses interest.
- Praise your child's efforts.

Fisher-Price® Preschool Workbook titles:

- EXPLORING MY WORLD
- I CAN LEARN
- LET'S FIND OUT
- READY FOR SCHOOL
- FUN WITH LEARNING
- GETTING STARTED
- ON THE ROAD TO LEARNING
- WATCH ME LEARN

ESSENTIAL SKILLS

Each chapter contains repetitive activities that have been designed to help children learn to sort, separate, put together, and figure out the organizational skills necessary for learning and thinking.

Chapter 1   Watch Me Practice My Skills

This chapter features basic readiness skills, such as visual discrimination, and activities that provide practice with small motor control.

Chapter 2   Watch Me Write

An action alphabet is featured in this chapter. Action verbs, such as *act*, *bake*, and *carry* are used instead of nouns. Children can practice writing upper and lower case letters and also associate each letter with its beginning sound.

Chapter 3   Watch Me Work with Sounds

Beginning consonant sounds and rhyming words are presented in this chapter. Activities that allow children to evaluate sounds and categorize them in groups are included.

Chapter 4   Watch Me Learn Math

Size comparisons and number sets are featured along with counting from one to twenty-five.

WATCH ME PRACTICE MY SKILLS

It's time to dress up!

Look closely at both pictures.

Then circle four things in the picture at the left that are missing from the picture at the right.

Skills: Recognizing differences; Noticing details

WATCH ME PRACTICE MY SKILLS

Look at each large picture.
Then look at the detail in each small box.
Find that detail in each large picture and circle it.

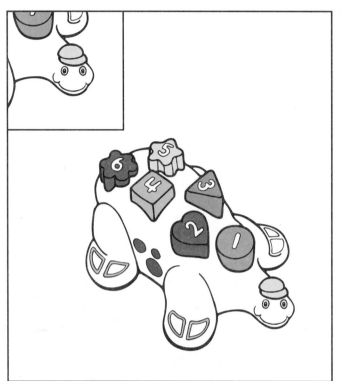

Skills: Visual discrimination; Noticing details

10

WATCH ME PRACTICE MY SKILLS

Look at each large picture.
Then look at the detail in each small box.
Find that detail in each large picture and circle it.

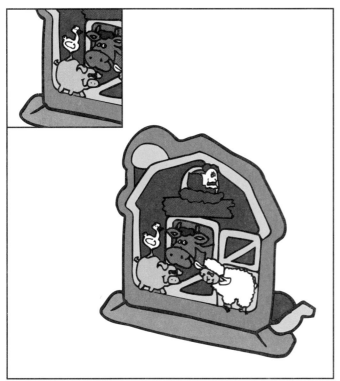

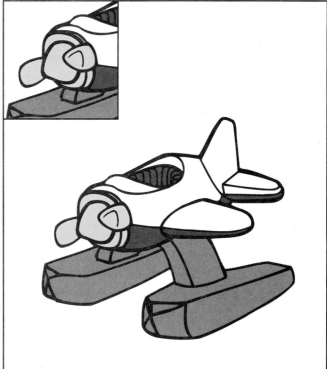

Skills: Visual discrimination; Noticing details

WATCH ME PRACTICE MY SKILLS

The knight is ready to joust.
Help him get to the arena.

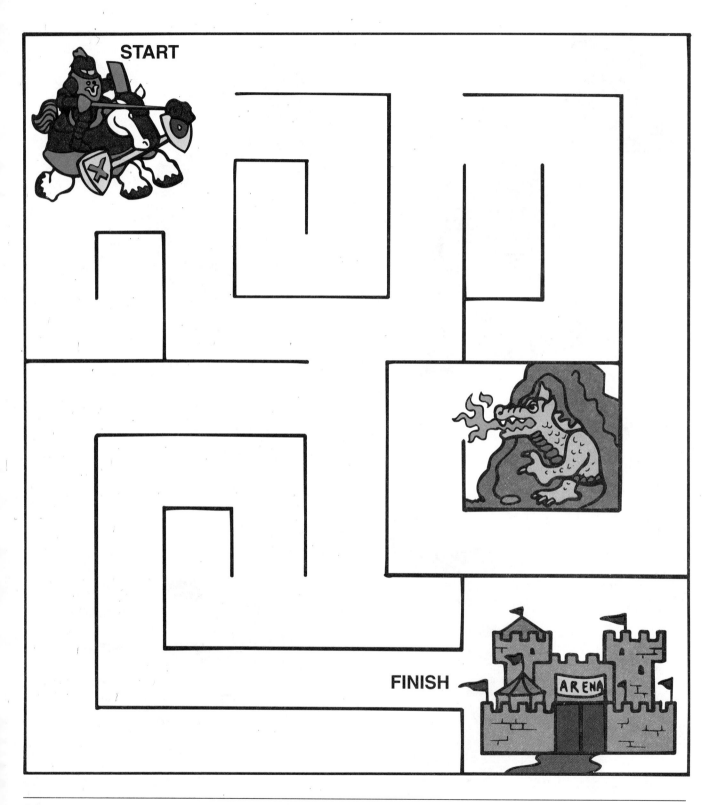

Skills: Visual perception; Fine motor skill development

WATCH ME PRACTICE MY SKILLS

Help the knight get to the dragon.

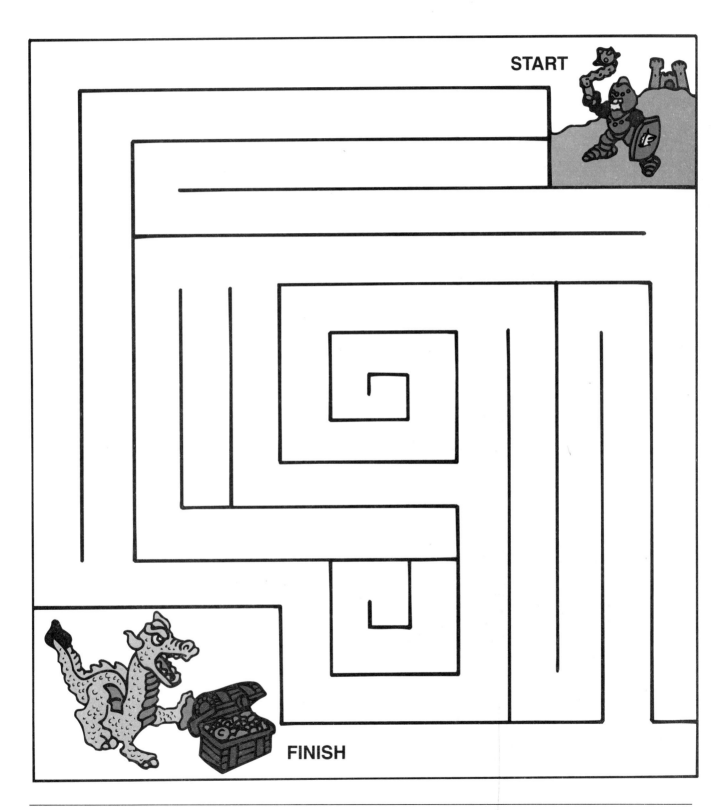

START

FINISH

Skills: Visual perception; Fine motor skill development

WATCH ME PRACTICE MY SKILLS

Who's ready to fight a fire?
Trace the broken lines to find out.

Skills: Fine motor skill development; Eye/hand coordination

WATCH ME PRACTICE MY SKILLS

Who works in a circus?
Trace the broken lines to find out.

Skills: Fine motor skill development; Eye/hand coordination

WATCH ME PRACTICE MY SKILLS

Will you throw him a fish?
He loves to make a big splash!
Connect the dots from **A** to **Z** to find out who he is.
Then finish coloring the picture.

Skills: Letter order; Recognizing upper case letters

WATCH ME PRACTICE MY SKILLS

Giddy-up!
Who can pull you in a cart?
Connect the dots from **a** to **z** to find out.
Then finish coloring the picture.

Skills: Letter order; Recognizing lower case letters

A a

It's fun to dress up and **act** like pirates.
Follow the direction of each arrow.
Then practice writing and saying each letter.

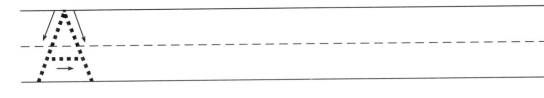

Skills: Writing upper/lower case "a"; Writing left to right; Saying letter sounds

WATCH ME WRITE

Bb

It's time to **bake** the gingerbread.
Follow the direction of each arrow.
Then practice writing and saying each letter.

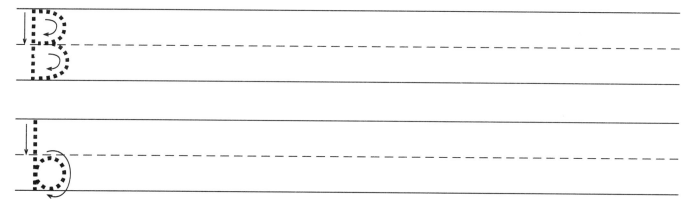

Skills: Writing upper/lower case "b"; Writing left to right; Saying letter sounds

WATCH ME WRITE

 C c

I'll **carry** the pails. Will you take the sand toys?
Follow the direction of each arrow.
Then practice writing and saying each letter.

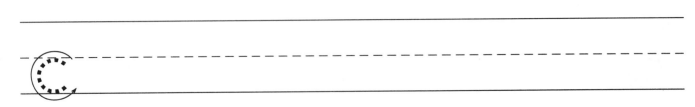

Skills: Writing upper/lower case "c"; Writing left to right; Saying letter sounds

20

©1997 Fisher-Price, Inc.

D d

Puppy likes to **dig** a hole and bury his bone.
Follow the direction of each arrow.
Then practice writing and saying each letter.

Skills: Writing upper/lower case "d"; Writing left to right; Saying letter sounds

E e

First, I'll **eat** my burrito; then the corn.
Follow the direction of each arrow.
Then practice writing and saying each letter.

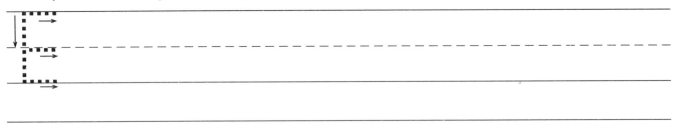

Skills: Writing upper/lower case "e"; Writing left to right; Saying letter sounds

F f

Baby likes me to **feed** her.
Follow the direction of each arrow.
Then practice writing and saying each letter.

Skills: Writing upper/lower case "f"; Writing left to right; Saying letter sounds

G g

Go! Get those speeders and give them a ticket!
Follow the direction of each arrow.
Then practice writing and saying each letter.

Skills: Writing upper/lower case "g"; Writing left to right; Saying letter sounds

Hh

My bear smiles when I **hug** him.
Follow the direction of each arrow.
Then practice writing and saying each letter.

Skills: Writing upper/lower case "h"; Writing left to right; Saying letter sounds

I i

I will **ice** these cupcakes.
Follow the direction of each arrow.
Then practice writing and saying each letter.

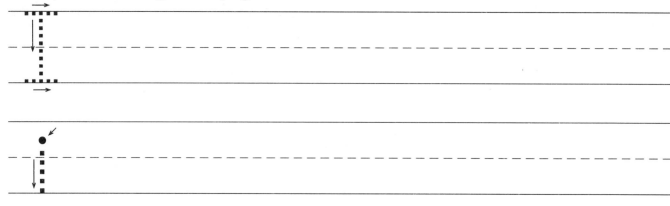

Skills: Writing upper/lower case "i"; Writing left to right; Saying letter sounds

J j

Watch the cow **jump** over the moon!
Follow the direction of each arrow.
Then practice writing and saying each letter.

Skills: Writing upper/lower case "j"; Writing left to right; Saying letter sounds

K k

Grandma **kisses** the baby.
Follow the direction of each arrow.
Then practice writing and saying each letter.

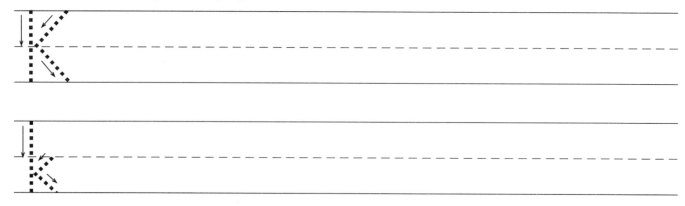

Skills: Writing upper/lower case "k"; Writing left to right; Saying letter sounds

L l

My Grandpa talks and I **listen**.
Follow the direction of each arrow.
Then practice writing and saying each letter.

Skills: Writing upper/lower case "l"; Writing left to right; Saying letter sounds

Mm

I am **mailing** a letter to my friend who moved away.
Follow the direction of each arrow.
Then practice writing and saying each letter.

Skills: Writing upper/lower case "m"; Writing left to right; Saying letter sounds

Nn

What shall we **name** the puppies? Perky is one good name. Can you think of others?
Follow the direction of each arrow.
Then practice writing and saying each letter.

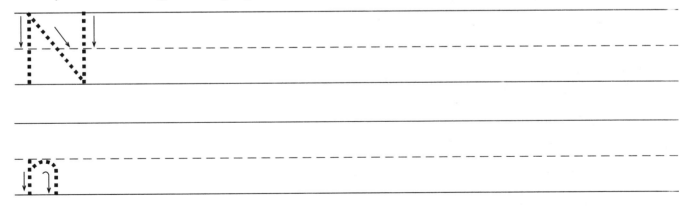

Skills: Writing upper/lower case "n"; Writing left to right; Saying letter sounds

O o

Did you **open** the door and let the cows out of the barn?
Follow the direction of each arrow.
Then practice writing and saying each letter.

Skills: Writing upper/lower case "o"; Writing left to right; Saying letter sounds

P p

The vendor will **push** his cart to the corner. What will you buy?
Follow the direction of each arrow.
Then practice writing and saying each letter.

Skills: Writing upper/lower case "p"; Writing left to right; Saying letter sounds

Q q

Quack! Quack! The duck will not stop quacking!
Follow the direction of each arrow.
Then practice writing and saying each letter.

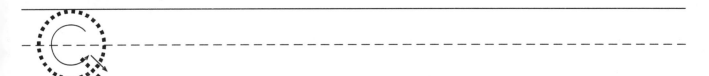

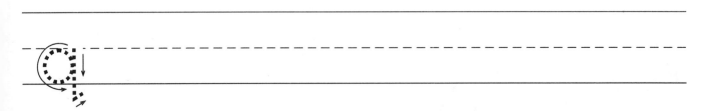

Skills: Writing upper/lower case "q"; Writing left to right; Saying letter sounds

R r

The girls like to **run** in a race.
Follow the direction of each arrow.
Then practice writing and saying each letter.

Skills: Writing upper/lower case "r"; Writing left to right; Saying letter sounds

S s

After we **set** the table, we can have tea!
Follow the direction of each arrow.
Then practice writing and saying each letter.

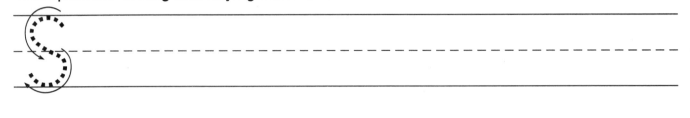

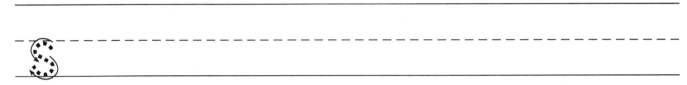

Skills: Writing upper/lower case "s"; Writing left to right; Saying letter sounds

WATCH ME WRITE

T t

Look! I can **tie** my shoelaces.
Follow the direction of each arrow.
Then practice writing and saying each letter.

Skills: Writing upper/lower case "t"; Writing left to right; Saying letter sounds

U u

It's time to **unload** the sand so we can build a sandcastle.
Follow the direction of each arrow.
Then practice writing and saying each letter.

Skills: Writing upper/lower case "u"; Writing left to right; Saying letter sounds

V v

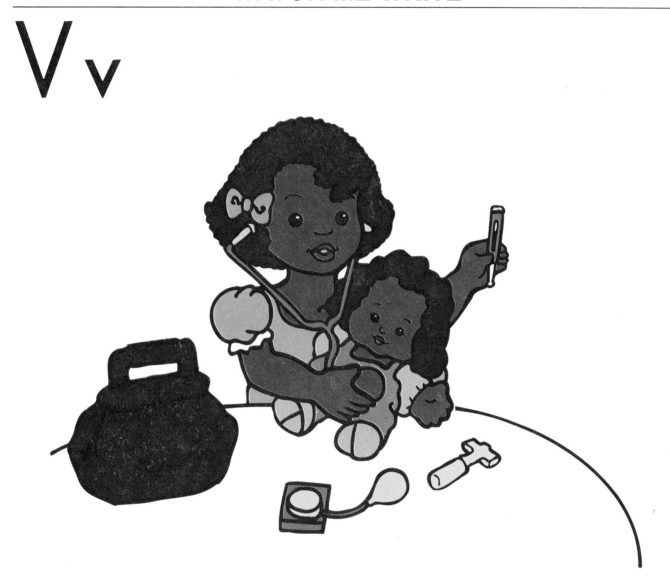

It's time to **visit** the doctor. Thump! Thump! Listen to the baby's heart.
Follow the direction of each arrow.
Then practice writing and saying each letter.

Skills: Writing upper/lower case "v"; Writing left to right; Saying letter sounds

W w

We love to **wear** jewelry when we go to a party. What will you wear?
Follow the direction of each arrow.
Then practice writing and saying each letter.

Skills: Writing upper/lower case "w"; Writing left to right; Saying letter sounds

X x

The doctor **x-rayed** my head and leg.
He said nothing is broken and I'll feel better soon.
Follow the direction of each arrow.
Then practice writing and saying each letter.

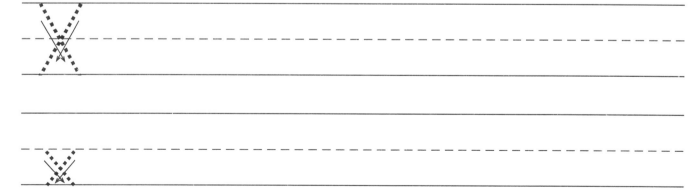

Skills: Writing upper/lower case "x"; Writing left to right; Saying letter sounds

The king **yells**, "Let the games begin!"
Then the knights begin to joust.
Follow the direction of each arrow.
Then practice writing and saying each letter.

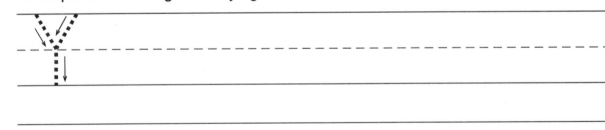

Skills: Writing upper/lower case "y"; Writing left to right; Saying letter sounds

Zz

It's time to **zip** up the sleeping bag and get some z's.
Follow the direction of each arrow.
Then practice writing and saying each letter.

Skills: Writing upper/lower case "z"; Writing left to right; Saying letter sounds

WATCH ME WORK WITH SOUNDS

Say the name of each picture.
Listen to its beginning sound.
Then circle all the pictures whose
names begin with the same sound as  "pail."

WATCH ME WORK WITH SOUNDS

Say the name of each picture.
Listen to its beginning sound.
Then circle all the pictures whose
names begin with the same sound as  "table."

WATCH ME WORK WITH SOUNDS

Say the name of each picture.
Listen to its beginning sound.
Then circle all the pictures whose
names begin with the same sound as  "saw."

Skills: Auditory and visual discrimination; Recognizing beginning sounds

WATCH ME WORK WITH SOUNDS

Say the name of each picture.
Listen to its beginning sound.
Then circle all the pictures whose
names begin with the same sound as  "dog."

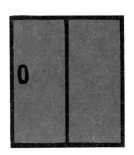

Skills: Auditory and visual discrimination; Recognizing beginning sounds

WATCH ME WORK WITH SOUNDS

Look at the first picture in each row and say its name.
Then say the name of the other pictures in that row.
Circle the picture whose name rhymes with the first one.

Skills: Auditory discrimination; Rhyming vocabulary

WATCH ME WORK WITH SOUNDS

Look at the first picture in each row and say its name.
Then say the name of the other pictures in that row.
Circle the picture whose name rhymes with the first one.

Skills: Auditory discrimination; Rhyming vocabulary

WATCH ME WORK WITH SOUNDS

Look at the first picture in each row and say its name.
Then say the name of the other pictures in that row.
Circle the picture whose name rhymes with the first one.

Skills: Auditory discrimination; Rhyming vocabulary

WATCH ME LEARN MATH

Which one is the smallest?
Look at the animals in each row.
Circle the one that is the **smallest**.

Skills: Comparing size

WATCH ME LEARN MATH

Say the name of each shape.

circle

rectangle

square

Color each circle.
Put an **X** on each rectangle.
Put a **line** under each square.

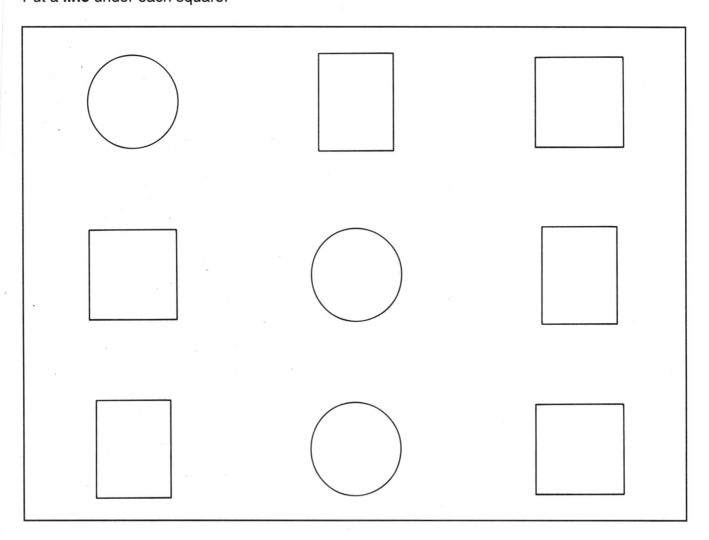

Skills: Recognizing shapes

WATCH ME LEARN MATH

Count the number of objects in each big box.
Trace the number in each small box.
Then finish coloring the pictures.

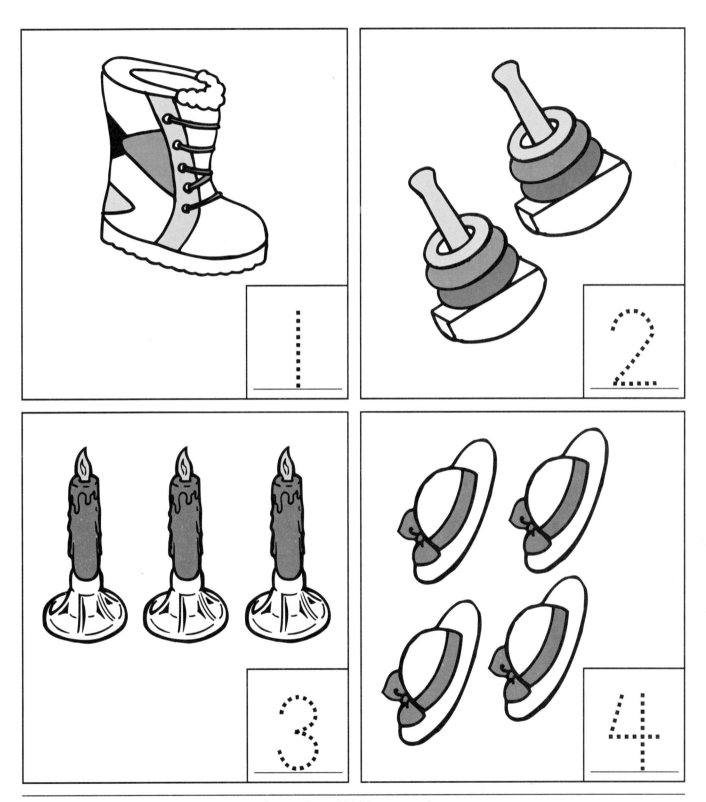

Skills: Identifying number sets; Counting; Writing numbers

WATCH ME LEARN MATH

Count the number of objects in each big box.
Trace the number in each small box.
Then finish coloring the pictures.

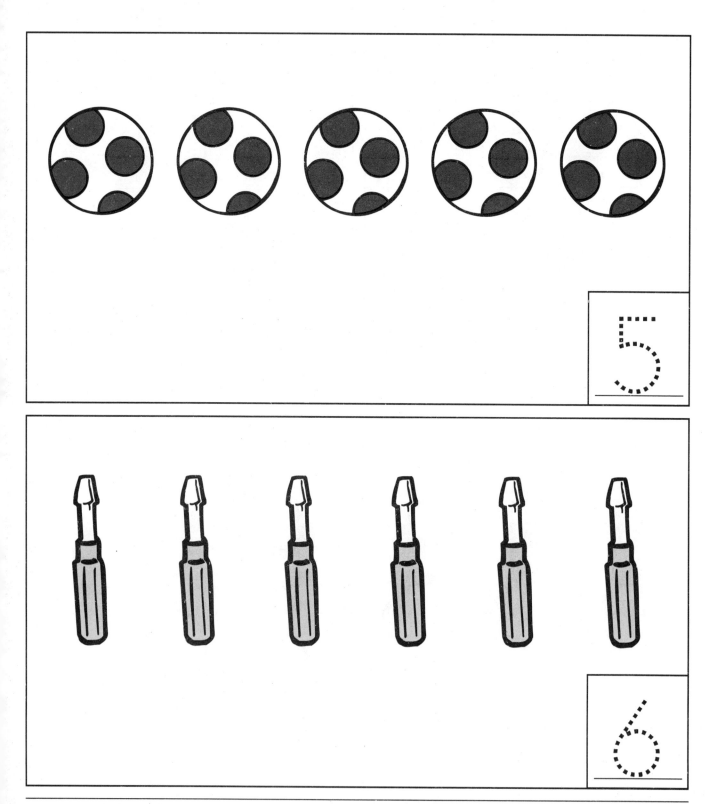

Skills: Identifying number sets; Counting; Writing numbers

WATCH ME LEARN MATH

Count the number of objects in each big box.
Trace the number in each small box.
Then finish coloring the pictures.

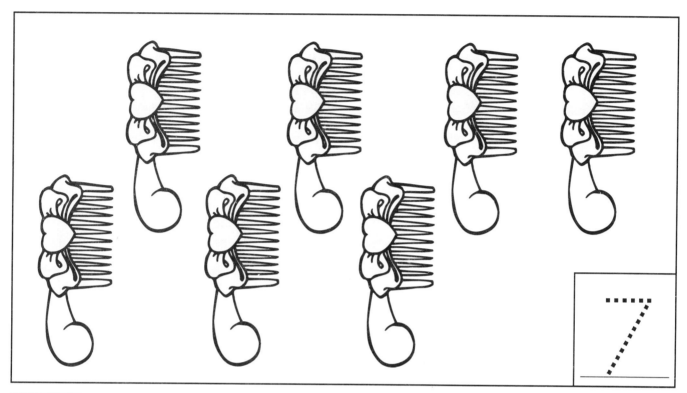

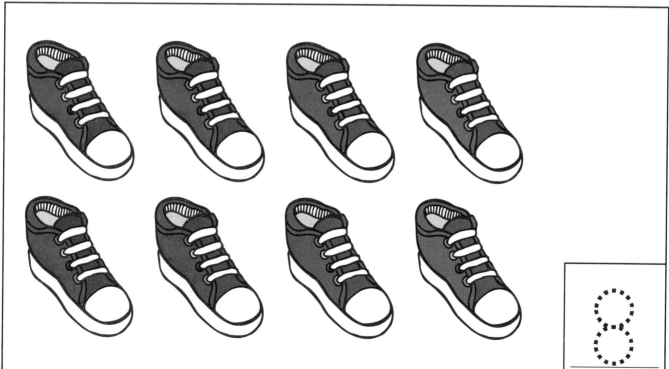

Skills: Identifying number sets; Counting; Writing numbers

WATCH ME LEARN MATH

Count the number of objects in each big box.
Trace the number in each small box.
Then finish coloring the pictures.

Skills: Identifying number sets; Counting; Writing numbers

WATCH ME LEARN MATH

Look at the sets in each box.
Circle the number that tells how many.

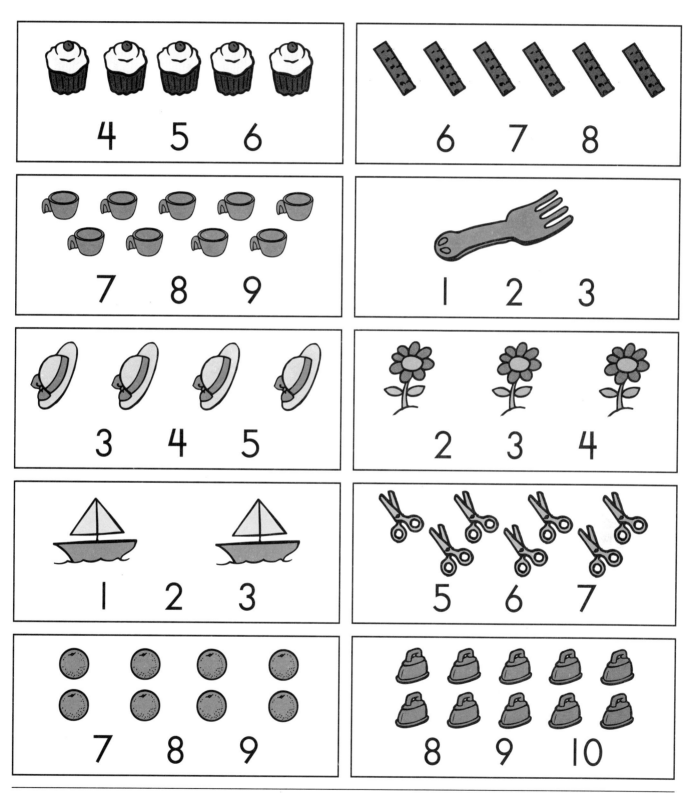

Skills: Recognizing sets of objects and the corresponding number

WATCH ME LEARN MATH

Let's go fishing!
Look at the pictures at the top of the page.
Count those objects in the large picture.
Then write how many.

fish   **fishing poles**   **worms**   **pails**

   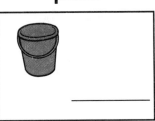

Skills: Counting sets of objects; Writing numbers

WATCH ME LEARN MATH

So many knights, ready to defend their castle.
Look at the pictures at the bottom of the page.
Count those objects in the large picture.
Then write how many.

Dragons	Knights	Yellow Swords	Ice Brigade

_____	_____	_____	_____

Skills: Counting sets of objects; Writing numbers

WATCH ME LEARN MATH

Can you count to **10**? Can you count to **20**?
Try counting to **25**.
Fill in the missing numbers.

1	2	3	___	5
6	___	8	___	___
11	12	___	14	15
16	___	18	___	20
21	22	___	24	___

Skills: Number order; Counting; Writing numbers

WATCH ME LEARN MATH

Let's go for a ride!
Follow the dots from **1** to **25** to find out what we'll ride in.
Then finish coloring the picture.

Skills: Number order; Recognizing numbers

WATCH ME LEARN MATH

Trouble at sea?
The rescue team is on its way!
Connect the dots from **1** to **25** to find out what the team rides in.

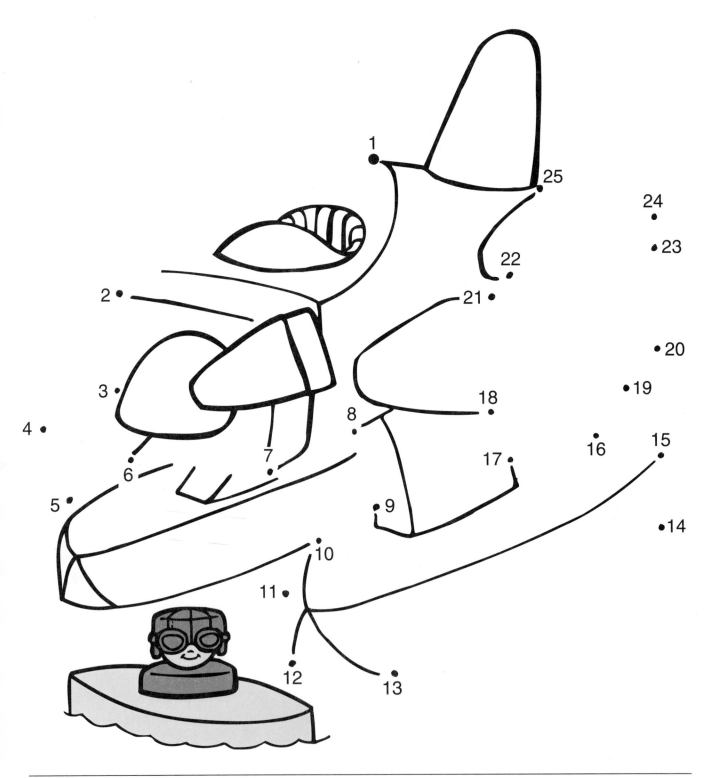

Skills: Number order; Recognizing numbers

WATCH ME LEARN MATH

Can you count **even** numbers?
Can you count **odd** numbers?
Fill in the missing numbers.

Even

2	4	6		10

Odd

	3		7	

Skills: Odd/Even number order; Counting; Writing numbers

WATCH ME LEARN MATH

Look at the pictures in each box.
Draw lines to connect each object on one side to an
object on the other side.

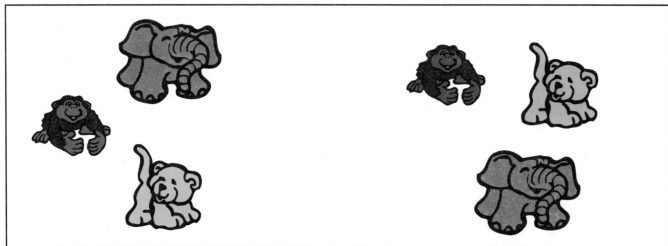

Skills: One-to-one correspondence

WATCH ME LEARN MATH

Look at the sets of pictures in each box.
Circle the set that shows **more.**
Put an **X** on the sets that show **less.**

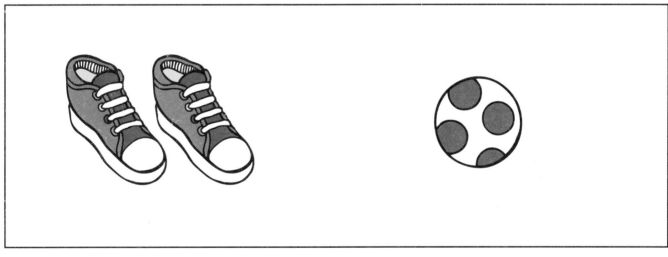

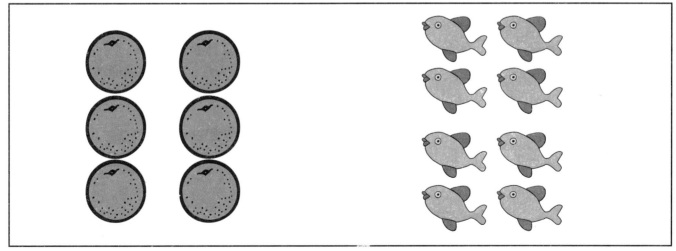

Skills: Identifying and comparing sets; Understanding more and less

ANSWER KEY

WATCH ME PRACTICE MY SKILLS

Look at the pictures.
Draw a line to connect the pictures that match.

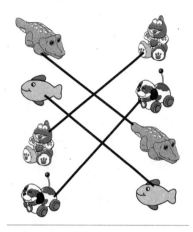

WATCH ME PRACTICE MY SKILLS

Let's visit the zoo!
Look at the animals on this page.
Draw lines to connect each baby to its parent.

WATCH ME PRACTICE MY SKILLS

It's time to play!
Look closely at both pictures.
Then circle four things at the top of the page that
are missing from the picture at the bottom.

WATCH ME PRACTICE MY SKILLS

It's time to dress up!
Look closely at both pictures.
Then circle four things in the picture at the left that
are missing from the picture at the right.

WATCH ME PRACTICE MY SKILLS

Look at each large picture.
Then look at the detail in each small box.
Find that detail in each large picture and circle it.

WATCH ME PRACTICE MY SKILLS

Look at each large picture.
Then look at the detail in each small box.
Find that detail in each large picture and circle it.

ANSWER KEY

Page 12

WATCH ME PRACTICE MY SKILLS

The knight is ready to joust.
Help him get to the arena.

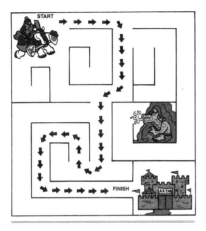

Page 13

WATCH ME PRACTICE MY SKILLS

Help the knight get to the dragon.

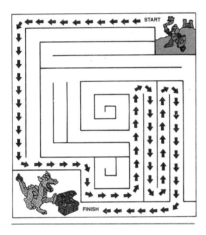

Page 16

WATCH ME PRACTICE MY SKILLS

Will you throw him a fish?
He loves to make a big splash!
Connect the dots from A to Z to find out who he is.
Then finish coloring the picture.

Page 17

WATCH ME PRACTICE MY SKILLS

Giddy-up!
Who can pull you in a cart?
Connect the dots from a to z to find out.
Then finish coloring the picture.

Page 44

WATCH ME WORK WITH SOUNDS

Say the name of each picture.
Listen to its beginning sound.
Then circle all the pictures whose
names begin with the same sound as "pail."

Page 45

WATCH ME WORK WITH SOUNDS

Say the name of each picture.
Listen to its beginning sound.
Then circle all the pictures whose
names begin with the same sound as "table."

ANSWER KEY

Page 46

WATCH ME WORK WITH SOUNDS

Say the name of each picture.
Listen to its beginning sound.
Then circle all the pictures whose
names begin with the same sound as "saw."

Page 47

WATCH ME WORK WITH SOUNDS

Say the name of each picture.
Listen to its beginning sound.
Then circle all the pictures whose
names begin with the same sound as "dog."

Page 48

WATCH ME WORK WITH SOUNDS

Look at the first picture in each row and say its name.
Then say the name of the other pictures in that row.
Circle the picture whose name rhymes with the first one.

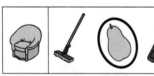

Page 49

WATCH ME WORK WITH SOUNDS

Look at the first picture in each row and say its name.
Then say the name of the other pictures in that row.
Circle the picture whose name rhymes with the first one.

Page 50

WATCH ME WORK WITH SOUNDS

Look at the first picture in each row and say its name.
Then say the name of the other pictures in that row.
Circle the picture whose name rhymes with the first one.

Page 51

WATCH ME LEARN MATH

Look at the two pictures in each box.
Circle the smaller picture.
Draw a line under the larger picture.

70

ANSWER KEY

Page 52

WATCH ME LEARN MATH

Which one is the largest?
Look at the animals in each row.
Circle the one that is the **largest**.

Page 53

WATCH ME LEARN MATH

Which one is the smallest?
Look at the animals in each row.
Circle the one that is the **smallest**.

Page 54

WATCH ME LEARN MATH

Say the name of each shape.

circle   rectangle   square

Color each circle.
Put an **X** on each rectangle.
Put a **line** under each square.

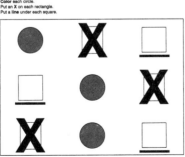

Page 59

WATCH ME LEARN MATH

Look at the sets in each box.
Circle the number that tells how many.

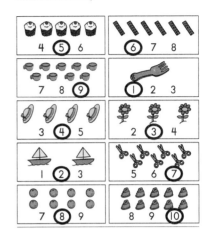

Page 60

WATCH ME LEARN MATH

Let's go fishing!
Look at the pictures at the top of the page.
Count those objects in the large picture.
Then write how many.

fish 6   fishing poles 2   worms 4   pails 4

Page 61

WATCH ME LEARN MATH

So many knights, ready to defend their castle.
Look at the pictures at the bottom of the page.
Count those objects in the large picture.
Then write how many.

Dragons 1   Knights 3   Yellow Swords 1   Ice Brigade 2

ANSWER KEY

Page 62

WATCH ME LEARN MATH

Can you count to **10**? Can you count to **20**?
Try counting to **25**.
Fill in the missing numbers.

1	2	3	4	5
6	7	8	9	10
11	12	13	14	15
16	17	18	19	20
21	22	23	24	25

Page 63

WATCH ME LEARN MATH

Let's go for a ride!
Follow the dots from **1** to **25** to find out what we'll ride in.
Then finish coloring the picture.

Page 64

WATCH ME LEARN MATH

Trouble at sea?
The rescue team is on its way!
Connect the dots from **1** to **25** to find out what the team rides in.

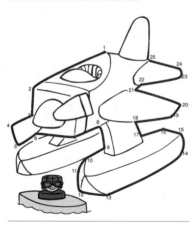

Page 65

WATCH ME LEARN MATH

Can you count **even** numbers?
Can you count **odd** numbers?
Fill in the missing numbers.

Even

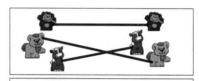

2	4	6	8	10

Odd

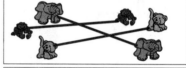

1	3	5	7	9

Page 66

WATCH ME LEARN MATH

Look at the pictures in each box.
Draw lines to connect each object on one side to an
object on the other side.

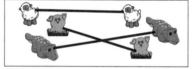

Page 67

WATCH ME LEARN MATH

Look at the sets of pictures in each box.
Circle the set that shows **more.**
Put an **X** on the sets that show **less.**

72

©1997 Fisher-Price, Inc.